End Game

End Game

Poems by

Laura J. Bobrow

© 2021 Laura J. Bobrow. All rights reserved.
This material may not be reproduced in any form, published,
reprinted, recorded, performed, broadcast,
rewritten or redistributed without
the explicit permission of Laura J. Bobrow.
All such actions are strictly prohibited by law.

Cover design by Shay Culligan

ISBN: 978-1-954353-86-2

Kelsay Books
502 South 1040 East, A-119
American Fork, Utah 84003

Susan Joan Raphael
1955–2021

*to our talented, beloved,
adventurous, extraordinary
Sooki*

Acknowledgments

In modified form, the following poems appeared in an earlier chapbook *Betrayed* (Finishing Line Press): "The Game's Not Over," "In the Tower of Babel," "Rites of Passage"

Other poems have appeared in:

Artemis Journal: "I Have Done My Best"
Magnapoets: "Within My Secret Garden"
Poet's Domain: "Considering Fingernails"
PSV Anthology: "July Morning"
Trinacria: "At the Final Table," "The Garden," "I Said It. So There.," "In the Mountains," "The Reckoning"

Contents

The Game's Not Over	11
At the Final Table	12
In the Mountains	13
Premonition	14
I Have Done My Best	15
Expulsion	16
Considering Fingernails	17
Miswritten	18
The Garden	19
Lottery	20
The Road's End	21
The Kiss	22
In the Tower of Babel	23
I Said It. So There.	24
Morning	25
End Game	26
Rapture	27
July Morning	28
Rites of Passage	29
Map Quest	30
The Reckoning	31
Silence	32

The Game's Not Over

I place the cards to play at solitaire.
Straight edge to edge they press me
    close around
and stare at me, the soldiers and the kings,
red queens and knaves, the saints and
    feudal lords.
Too bad, my friend, a joker calls out loud.
Play out your luck, but then you forfeit all,
for win or lose or draw, you'll wind up dead.

Not yet, I say. *I am my daddy's child,*
and he lived long, and healthy for his years.
I'll quit, he said, when every card is played.
He kept the ace of spades beneath his sleeve.

At the Final Table

My chance to beat the odds is lost, I fear.
Although I've used each strategy I know,
the way to cheat on death is still unclear.

My nest egg's spent. It's all or nothing here.
Beginner's luck was used up long ago.
That chance to beat the odds is gone, I fear.

I've tried. I've bet the maximum each year.
I've studied every card in the tableau.
The way to cheat on death is still unclear.

The stakes are high now that the end is near.
I still hunt for a gamester's edge, although
my chance to beat the odds is lost, I fear.

Too soon I'll have to face the Big Cashier.
It's true, but I keep hoping, even so,
the way to cheat on death might still
    come clear.

I'm on my knees. And God knows
    I'm sincere.
I need to find a prayer that's apropos.
The chance to stack the deck is gone, I fear,
and how to cheat on death is still unclear.

In the Mountains

I clamber to the topmost rocks and pause.
No traffic noise can reach me at this height.
The sound of snowfall dripping as it thaws
Half muffles the shrill "kee-yah" of a kite,

Enfolding me in shivers of delight.
My eyes are fixed on edges clean and hard.
Old fears of death which torment me I might,
Upon this mesa, finally discard.

Nirvana. I inhale its peace unmarred.
Too soon a voice intrudes. It's low and gruff
And deftly finds its way behind my guard.
It scoffs, *You can't stay here. Come off
   your bluff.*

*Now trudge back to the plain where
   you belong.*
Some say it is bewitched,
   the mountain's song.

Premonition

The prescient trees have come awake.
They turn their leaves up to the sky.
There is a storm about to break.

In fear the speckled rattlesnake
seeks shelter where the earth is dry.
The prescient trees have come awake.

I still have old amends to make.
The time is short, and I may die
within this storm about to break.

My limbs are weak. My innards shake.
The years have passed too quickly by.
The prescient trees have come awake

and now, as dark mists overtake
my vision, I cannot deny:
the final storm is soon to break.

I wish that I might yet forsake
those thunderous clouds. But though I try,
the prescient trees have come awake.
There is a storm about to break.

I Have Done My Best

A blotch of distant color in an otherwise
    clear sky
portends a storm of superlative dimensions.
An almost imperceptible rumble beneath the
    earth's crust
is predictive of an event of world-shattering
    devastation.

Confusion, disarray, bedlam,
cataclysmic occurrences tremble on the brink
at every moment of every day.
But I have done my best.

I have not opened my umbrella inside
    the house.
I have not stepped on a crack nor walked
    beneath a ladder.
I wear garlic and carry a rabbit's foot.
I have turned seven times clockwise.

My cricket chirps on the hearth.

Expulsion

I have barricaded myself
behind books and comforters.
At any moment the earth
will relinquish gravity.

I will scatter into the cosmos,
never to reassemble.
Goodbye to the creases in my earlobes.
Goodbye to my insy bellybutton.

Gone. Poof!
Just like that.
If I hold on tight to the cat
maybe we can travel together.

Considering Fingernails

We scratched pictures onto frosted windows
those first cold-enough mornings.
Summers we dug deep into the skin of
    oranges
to reach the pulpy prize within.
Late into the night we plucked at guitar
    strings,
danced licentious glissades across prickly
    insect bites.

You molded your hardness against my
    vulnerable flesh
and I chewed at your keratoid excrescence.
You, my symbiotic joy, can break and
    grow again.
I will merely break and die.

I weep for you.

Miswritten

I was born in a million pieces
like letters in a printer's tray.
My patch of parchment
seethed with endless possibilities.

And then I pieced together a life.
No, I want to shout, *it was wrong.*
That is not who I really was at all.
I let caution muddle the syntax.

And now it is too late to rewrite
and perilously close to the deadline.

The Garden

The Creeping Jenny has not crept,
misplanted where the kitten slept.
Though pictures showed it lush and big,
Hibiscus bush remains a twig.

Life's garden that I wished to sow
perversely has refused to grow,
has suffered, has become distraught,
has withered and has come to naught.

Lottery

The ultimate game piece dangles
just beyond my breath.
Lord, let me be an Instant Winner.

Master of Statistical Probability, it is I,
who have never won, even a raffle.
See how precisely
I scratch at the film with yellow,
scabrous nails.

Impartial Judge, whose decision is final,
you can keep the All-Expenses-Paid-Trip-
    for-Two.
All I want is a deferral.

The Road's End

I drive across a mountain ridge
and take the road down to the shore.
I cross a shaky wooden bridge
that I have never seen before.

Stark trees rear high on either side.
A rising mist obscures my sight.
I clench my teeth, and bleary-eyed
drive grimly through the endless night.

A mausoleum's in my way.
I enter it, though not by will.
The journey's over, voices say
and laugh with a sepulchral chill.

And so it is, and so must be
when other roads are closed to me.

The Kiss

I wish I had never met Death.
I wish we had never become acquainted.
I could go on imagining Heaven
    easily obtained,
a delightful stroll along an astral beach.

But I have seen him up close.
He will surround me with putrid fumes.
His lips will crush my lips
and leave a bad taste in my mouth.

I will emerge gasping for breath
and nowhere near the shore.

In the Tower of Babel

In the utmost top of the ziggurat
I sit in front of a cavernous hearth,
wine goblet in hand,
murmuring indecipherable words
to my lone companion,
my prince of love,
who cannot understand me.

This hearth will be my sepulcher,
a monument to my wasted breath.
Only ash where there should be flame,
only fallen bricks to cover me.

I Said It. So There.

That is how the matter stands.
I've wished it back a hundredfold.
The time is past for reprimands.

The deed is now out of my hands.
Of course you have the right to scold,
but done is done. The matter stands.

One word exudes a thousand strands.
Once out, they travel uncontrolled,
The time is past for reprimands.

Rescinding's done in fairylands.
We can but watch the tale unfold.
And that is how the matter stands.

I cannot cede to your demands
though I am coaxed, compelled, cajoled.
The time is past for reprimands.

Though I've regrets, the crime expands,
and I am tired, and I am old.
Too bad, but thus the matter stands.
The time's way past for reprimands.

Morning

Damp
pillows
tossed aside,
testifying
to a night spent in
mystifying dreamscapes,
admixtures of place and time,
reappearance of those long dead
whose voices beckon me the sleeper
not to wake but to succumb and follow.

End Game

Red Rover, Red Rover, it's time to
    cross over,
Mother, may I go?
My playmates have left me. The schoolyard
    is empty.
I'm left here alone in the snow.

I could use my jump rope to try to cross over.
Is that how it's done? I don't know.
My loved ones are waiting. I might play
    at leapfrog.
but no one is nearby. Hello?

Red Light or Green Light. I need to
    cross over.
I'm ready to do it although
I'm blindfolded, groping. And if I reach
    home free
I may not come back. That is so.

Rapture

Repetitive shapes, confluent shadows
expand, shift, dodge.
Light shines in from a far distant corridor.

Eyes tight closed, arms clutching emptiness,
spinning, caroming,
I make my escape.

July Morning

I am getting ready to know how
I am going to feel after I am dead.
I guess that chocolate won't matter any more
but the sound of the mower and the clip clop
    of Bessie, the milkman's horse
and the chirring of cicadas,
will.

When my body lies dissected,
unsheathed onto Formica,
when my credit cards have been clipped
    in half,
what do you suppose will have happened
to the Gettysburg Address?
to my telephone number?
to the songs in my head?

Rites of Passage

I have not yet decided whether to be buried,
burned, tied in a sack and tossed into
    the ocean,
or placed in a tree to let the sun bleach
    my bones.
Set up a signpost and turn my face in
    the direction
I must go.

Mangu ruled heavily. When later he
    was killed
he was borne by his followers to the royal
    cemetery.
Buried with him were servants, horses,
    and wives.
His was a fine funeral. Of those who
    encountered his cortege,
all were slain.

My death will be a mere disturbance.
Placing forehead against forehead,
    mourners will weep in pairs.
I do not expect that there will be a
    yoghurt-sipping ceremony
at my grave.

Map Quest

I'm new to this dying and yet I must say
it seems only fair nature show her intent
by lighting a pathway for me to pursue.
How else shall I locate those great gilded
    halls?

With what fragrant bark should my feet now
    be shod?
In what new-made cloth should my body
    be dressed?
I fear I will seem like an alien soul
who's blundered unknowingly into the ball
where revelers dance to the trumpeters' blare
in suitable wingéd attire.

The Reckoning

When it comes time to reckon up my day,
the time to balance figures bright and grim,
offenses, crimes, transgressions will
    outweigh
whatever virtues filled the interim.

Though possibly you will not see my face,
I'll do my best to rectify the tales.
While I lie dormant in a nameless place
my thumb will gently rest upon the scales.

Silence

Count again the soundless things:
smoke rising from a smoldering fire,
cotton thread that stitched a shroud,
the stone that bears a given name,
sculptured birds that guard a grave,
the owl that seeks it prey at night.

Dark spiders spin their silent webs.
There are no words for loss

About the Author

Laura is an acclaimed professional storyteller as well as a prize-winning poet whose work has been published internationally.

www.laurajbobrow.com

www.ingramcontent.com/pod-product-compliance
Lightning Source LLC
Chambersburg PA
CBHW021029090426
42738CB00007B/950